DOG ON A LOG®
Chapter Books
Step 2

DOG ON A LOG Books
Tucson, Arizona

Copyright ©2017 By Pamela Brookes
All Rights Reserved.
For information, contact the publisher at
read@dogonalogbooks.com

Public Domain images from
www.clker.com

The Hat and Bug Shop
Public domain cover photo from
www.publicdomainpictures.net

ISBN: 978-1949471014

www.dogonalogbooks.com

FIVE
CHAPTER BOOKS
2

(A Collection of Five Books)

By Pamela Brookes

Download DOG ON A LOG printable gameboards, games, flashcards, and other activities at:
www.dogonalogbooks.com/printables.

Parents and Teachers:
Receive email notifications of new books and printables. Sign up at:
www.dogonalogbooks.com/subscribe

Table of Contents

DOG ON A LOG

Parent and Teacher Guides

General information
on Dyslexia and
Struggling Readers

The Author's Routine
for Teaching Reading

Book 1. *Teaching a Struggling Reader: One Mom's Experience with Dyslexia*

Book 2. *How to Use Decodable Books to Teach Reading*

Available for free from many online booksellers or read at:
www.dogonalogbooks.com/free

MUD ON THE PATH

Bob the Dog

Bob is a big dog. A big tan dog. He can pick up thick logs. He can sit and set his chin on the bed. He can get in the back of the van when he wants.

Bob is my pal. If I am sad, he will kiss my chin. He will get the ball when I toss it. He sits on the rug with me. I rub his back and neck.

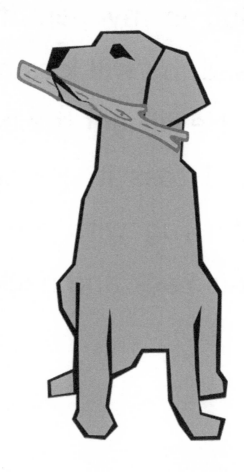

Bob is a big dog.

The Log Hut

Dad said Bob and I could pick up logs. I would pick up a log. Bob would jog with it to Dad. Dad cut the logs. He set log on top of log. Then he fit the logs with pegs. The logs got tall.

The logs are a hut. The hut is for me and Bob. The log hut is in the dip in the hills. The hut has a top. It can not get wet in the hut.

The hut is for me and Bob.

When Bob and I are in the hut, Dad is at the top of the hill. If I yell to Dad, he will get us pop and chips. Bob likes chips. He does not like pop. He does not like that pop goes fizz. I like that pop has fizz.

The Nap

Dad let Bob and me nap in the hut. I got up from the nap. Bob was not in the hut.

The hut was in fog. Fog was in the dip in the hills. Fog was on top of the hill.

I had to yell, "Bob, Bob, get to the hut." Bob did not get to the hut.

I ran to Dad. "Bob is not in the hut. Bob is not in the dip in the hills," I said.

Bob was not in the hut.

"Let us go get Bob," Dad said. "You and I can jog on the path and call for Bob."

The Path

Dad got his back pack. He and I ran on the path. The path was wet. The path had mud. A log was on the path. I did not see the log. I hit the log and fell in the mud. I got mud on my leg and a rip in my top.

The fog was thick. Dad did not see that I fell. Dad fell on the log. Dad got mud on his chin and lip.

"Are you OK?" Dad said.

"I am OK, but I do not see Bob," I said.

"Bob, Bob. Get to the hut," I did yell.

Bob did not yip back. I was sad.

A Tan Cub

The path got big. It had lots of mud. Dad and I could not jog or run. Dad sat on a log. I sat on a rock. "What is that?" I said.

A tan cub was on a log. "Does it have a mom?" I said.

"It should," Dad said. "A cub wants to be with his mom."

"Will you or I get a gash from the cub?" I said.

A tan cub was on a log.

"Not if you sit and do not run," Dad said.

Dad and I sat. Dad did not run. I did not jog. Dad and I sat and sat and sat.

The cub's mom ran to the cub. I could see the mom lick the cub. Then they ran on the path into the hills.

"Did the mom kiss the cub?" I said.

"Yes," said Dad. "The mom likes her cub. The mom likes to kiss her cub."

"Can we go get Bob?" I said to Dad.

"Yes. The mom and the cub are up the hill. It is OK for us to jog and run," Dad said.

Sad

Dad and I ran, but we could not see Bob. Dad said, "Let us go back to the hut."

When we got to the hut, Bob was not in it.

"I am sad," I said to dad. "I want to see Bob."

"Let me hug you," Dad said.

Dad and I had a hug. Then Dad said, "We will call to Bob. He will get to the hut if we call him."

"Let me hug you," Dad said.

"Bob, Bob," Dad did yell.

"Bob, Bob," I did yell.

Bob did not get to the hut.

At the Hut

Dad and I sat in the hut. Dad got chips from his back pack. Dad got pop from his back pack.

I did not want pop. I did not want the pop to fizz.

"Let us have chips and pop," Dad said. "Then we can go back on the path and call to Bob."

Dad had pop. I had chips. Then we got on the path to call for Bob.

Mud on the Path

The path had lots of mud. The mud was thick. The mud was up my leg. The mud was not fun.

"Could Bob be in the mud?" I said to Dad.

"He could be. But I bet he is not sad. I bet the mud is fun for him."

Dad and I got on the path. "Do not run into that log," I said to Dad.

The path had lots of mud.

"I will not," said Dad. "I do not want to hit the log. I do not want to cut my leg."

"I want to jog, but the mud is thick," I said.

"It is OK. We can get on the big rock and call to Bob," Dad said.

The Big Rock

Dad got on the rock. I got on the rock. It was big. I did not want to fall. "Bob, Bob. We are on the rock," I did yell.

"Yip. Yip, yip, yip."
It was Bob. Bob ran on
the path to us. Bob got
on the rock. "Yip, yip,
yip."

It was Bob.

Bob

I was not sad. Bob was on the rock. Bob was with us. Bob had mud on his leg and back and lip. Bob got mud on Dad. "It is OK," Dad said. "Bob can get mud on us."

"Let me hug you," I said to Bob. He sat for a hug. Then I got a kiss on my chin from Bob. The kiss had mud. Bob got mud on my chin. That was OK. Bob was with us.

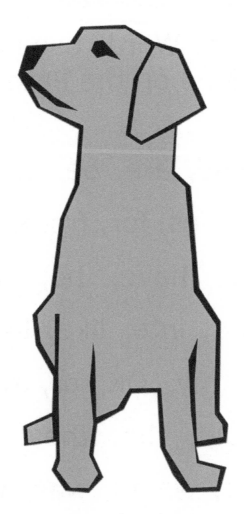

He sat for a hug

Sight Words used in "Mud on the Path"

a, and, are, be, could, do, does, for, from, go, goes, have, he, her, his, I, into, like, likes, me, my, OK, or, said, should, the, they, to, want, wants, was, we, when, would

Approximately 1,000 total words

THE RED HEN

Do You Want A Hen?

"Jan, do you want to get a hen?" Mom says.

"Yes, I do," Jan says. "Can she be a big red hen?"

"If the shop has a big red hen," Mom says. "Let us go to the shop. Let us see what hens they have."

Jan and her mom get in the van. They have a box in the back for the hen they will get.

Jan and her mom get in the van.

"This will be fun. Let us go to the hen shop," Mom says.

"To get a big red hen," Jan says.

Sam's Hen and Chick Shop

The man in the shop has a red cap. On the cap is, "**Sam's Hen and Chick Shop.**"

In the shop is a hat rack. The rack has lots of caps.

Red caps and tan caps. The caps all say, **"Sam's Hen and Chick Shop."**

"Are you Sam?" Mom says.

On the cap is, *"**Sam's Hen and Chick Shop.**"*

"I am. What can I do for you?" says Sam.

"I would like a big red hen," says Jan. "A hen that wants to have chicks."

"Do you want to have chicks?" Sam says to Mom.

"Yes. We have 5 hens but would like to have ten. A hen that wants to have 4 chicks would be fun. The mom hen and her chicks could be in a nest in the pen," says Mom.

"We could see the mom hen and the chicks sit in the sun. They can dig in the mud. We could see the chicks get fed. The chicks would get big, big, big. Then we would have ten hens," says Jan.

Sam, Mom, and Jan go to the back of the shop. Lots of hens sit in a pen.

"I would like that big red hen," says Jan. "Does she want to have chicks?"

"Yes," says Sam. "She likes to sit on eggs. She would like to have chicks."

Mom gets the box from the van. Sam sets the hen in the box. Mom gets Sam cash for the hen.

Sam sets the box with the hen in the back of the van. "Have fun with your hen," says Sam.

"I will," says Jan.

Gal Pals

In the van Jan says, "I will call her Miss Sal. She and I will be gal pals."

From the box in the back of the van, Miss Sal says, "Bock, bock, bock."

"She likes for you to call her Miss Sal," says Mom.

She and I will be gal pals.

The Hen Pen

The van is at the hen pen.

"Let us get the box with Miss Sal and set it in the pen," says Mom.

Jan and Mom get the box. They get the hen from the back of the van. They set it in the pen. Miss Sal hops from the box. The 5 hens run up to see the red hen.

"They will be pals," Jan says. "But I will be her gal pal."

The 5 hens run up to see the red hen.

"Could she have a bath?" Jan says.

"Hens do not like baths," says Mom.

"I wish she would like a bath. It would be fun for her to have a bath," says Jan.

"It would be fun for you, but not for Miss Sal," says Mom. "I bet she would like to have a bug. Do you see bugs for her?"

Jan picks up a log. "Here is a bug. Here are lots of bugs," she says. "Here chick, chick. Here are bugs for you."

The hens run when Jan says, "Here chick, chick." They can see the bugs at the log.

"Yum, yum," says Mom. "Lots of bugs for the hens."

"Yuck," says Jan. "I would not like bugs."

"You are not a hen," Mom says.

The Nest

Miss Sal and the hens get to be pals. Then Miss Sal sits on a nest of eggs.

"She will sit on the eggs. She will sit and sit. Then she will have chicks," Mom says.

"When will she have chicks?" Jan says.

Then Miss Sal sits on a nest of eggs.

"She will have to sit and sit. Then we will see the chicks. Miss Sal will be in the nest with the chicks. Then she will let them dig in the mud," Mom says

When the sun is up Jan goes to see Miss Sal. Miss Sal sits on the eggs. She does not have chicks.

Miss Sal does not have chicks when the sun sets. Jan goes to bed.

Then the sun is up. Jan runs to the pen. Miss Sal sits on the eggs. She does not have chicks. The sun sets and Jan goes to bed. Miss Sal does not have chicks yet.

Jan is sad. Miss Sal does not have chicks.

Mom says, "She will have chicks. The sun has to go up then set lots and lots. Then she will have chicks."

4 Chicks

Jan goes to the pen. She is sad Miss Sal does not have chicks.

"Pip," says a chick.

"Pip," says Miss Sal.

"You have chicks!" Jan says. "Miss Sal, you have 4 chicks."

Jan runs up the hill.

"Mom, Mom," Jan calls.

Mom is at the dish tub. She has a dish in the suds. She sets the dish back in the tub. "What is it?" Mom says.

"Miss Sal has chicks," Jan says. "Do you want to see them?"

"Yes, I do," says Mom.

"She has 4 chicks."

Jan and Mom run to the pen. All the hens sit at the nest. They want to see the chicks. Jan and Mom can not see Miss Sal.

"Git, git, go" says Mom to the hens.

Jan and Mom can see Miss Sal. They can see the nest. They can see 4 chicks.

"She has chicks," Mom says. "She has 4 chicks."

"Pip," say the chicks.

"Pip," says Miss Sal.

Miss Sal hops from the nest. The chicks hop from the nest. Miss Sal digs in the mud. The chicks dig in the mud.

Jan picks up a log. "Here are bugs," she says.

Miss Sal and the chicks run to the bugs.

"Yum, yum for chicks," says Mom.

"Yuck, I do not like bugs," Jan says. "But I like that we have chicks."

"I like that I have a kid," says Mom. "You will get big, big, big."

"But I will not like bugs when I am big, big, big," says Jan.

"I want to hug you," Mom says to Jan.

"Pip," Miss Sal says to her chicks.

Sight Words used in "The Red Hen"

a, and, are, be, could, do, does, eggs, for, from, go, goes, has, have, her, here, I, is, like, likes, nest, of, say, says, see, she, the, they, to, want, wants, we, what, would, you, your

Approximately 1,025 total words

THE
HAT AND BUG SHOP

Do You Want a Bug?

Jan and her mom sit in a shop. It is **The Hat and Bug Shop.**

The Hat and Bug Shop has pop in cups for pals. They can sip the pop when they shop. They get to see the hats. Then they get to sip pop from cups.

"Do you want a hat?" Mom says to Jan.

"I want to get a red hat," Jan says to her mom.

"Do you want to get a bug?" Mom says.

"Will it hop?" Jan says.

"It could," says Mom. "It could hop from the box on to your hat."

"It could hop from the box on to your hat."

"Do they have bugs that do not hop?" says Jan.

"Let us go see," Mom says.

The Hat Man

Jan and Mom go see the man. He is in the back of the shop.

"I would like to get a red hat. I would like a bug that does not hop," Jan says to the man.

"OK," the man says. "But I do not have red hats. You can get a hat with a ball on top. Or you can get a hat that has a sun on it. You can get a hat that has a bat on it."

"A bat hat?" Mom says

"Yes. A bat hat. I had a hat that says, 'Sam's Hen and Chick Shop.' I do not have it here. Sam has it at his shop."

I had a hat that says, 'Sam's Hen and Chick Shop.'

The Box

A tan box sits on a rack. Jan gets the box to see what is in it. It has a bug and a rat. The bug is on the rat. "Does the bug like the rat?" Jan says to the man.

"Yes. They are pals," the man says.

"Does the bug like the rat?" Jan says to the man.

"I would like to get the bug and rat. I would like to be pals with the bug and rat. Can I get them?"

"You can not get the bug and rat. I will not sell them to you. They are for the shop. They like it here."

The bug falls from the box on to the rug.

"That is bad. The bug is on the rug. What can I do to get the bug into the box?" Jan says.

"You can not get the bug. The rat will get the bug," the man says.

Get in The Box

The rat runs from the box. It runs to the bug. The bug gets on the rat. The rat runs to the back of the rack.

"Will they go into the box?" Jan says.

"They should," says the hat man. "The rat and bug have to get in the box or it will be bad."

The man gets the box. "Get in the box," he says to the rat.

The bug sits on the rat's neck. The rat runs from the man.

The rat runs to a hat. He nips the hat. The rat does not like the hat.

The rat runs to a hat that is like a cat. The rat nips the cat hat. Then the rat has a big nip.

"The rat likes to nip the cat hat," says Jan.

"The rat likes to nip the cat hat," says Jan.

"The rat can not nip the cat hat. The rat can not nip the bat hat. The cat can not nip this hat or that hat. RAT, DO NOT NIP THE HATS," the man says.

The bug hops from the rat. It runs to the man. It hops on the man's leg.

"Do not hop on my leg," the man says. "I do not like the bug on my leg. It is bad when the bug is on my leg. I want the bug to get into the box."

The man sits on the rug. He does not like the bug on his leg.

Jan picks up the bug. She sets it in the box.

"I like that you did that," the man says.

Pals

The rat hops on the man's back. It runs up to his neck. Then the rat does kiss the man on the chin.

"You are my pal," the man says to the rat. He sets the rat in the box. The bug gets on the rat. Then the bug gets on the rat's neck. He sits on the rat.

"Do you have hats for the rat and bug?" Jan says.

"I do not," the man says. "I have big hats and bat hats and cat hats. But I do not have rat or bug hats."

The man gets the rat from the box. He does kiss the rat.

"Will you kiss the bug?" Jan says.

The man gets the rat from the box. He does kiss the rat.

"Yuck," says the man. "I do not like to kiss bugs. I do not like bugs."

"You do not like bugs but you have **The Hat and Bug Shop**," Jan says.

"I like the rat. The rat likes bugs. I have bugs to be pals with the rat," the man says.

"I get that," Jan says. "You want to be pals with the rat. You get bugs for the rat. You are all pals."

"Yes," the man says.

"I like that," Mom says. "We would like to get a hat then we will go."

"I do not want to go," Jan says. "I like **The Hat and Bug Shop.**"

"I like **The Hat and Bug Shop**," Mom says to Jan, "but I bet the man, rat, and bug want to nap."

"Yes. We would like to nap," the man says. "What hat would you like to get?"

"I would like a red hat. You do not have a red hat. Can I get a hat with a sun on it?"

"Yes," the man says. "I have a hat like that."

Jan puts on the sun hat.

Mom says, "I like your hat."

"Can I pet your rat and bug?" Jan says to the man.

"Yes, you can," the man says.

Jan gets the box with the rat and bug. She pets the rat and the bug.

"Let us go," Mom says. "The man, rat, and bug want to nap."

Jan and her mom go from the shop. "When the man gets a red hat, I want to go back to get it."

"Yes. We can do that," Mom says.

Sight Words used in "The Hat and Bug Shop"

a, and, are, be, could, do, does, for, from, go, have, he, her, here, his, I, into, is, like, likes, my, of, OK, or, puts, says, see, she, should, the, they, to, want, we, what, would, you, your

Approximately 990 total words

BABS THE 'BOT

The 'Bot Kit

Mom and I got a 'bot kit at the 'bot shop. It had a tin can, rods, and lug nuts.

Mom and I fit the rods in the can. Then she and I fit the rods in the lug nuts. The kit was fun. 'Bots are fun.

A 'bot is a can with legs. I will call my 'bot Babs. She can not run. She can not jog. But she can hop on her legs. She can say, "Bip, bop, dop."

I will call my 'bot Babs.

A 'Bot That Mops

Mom wants Babs to mop. If dip and pop fall on the mat, Babs can mop them up.

Babs can mop with a wet mop. She can mop with a mop that is not wet. Mom does not like to mop. Mom says it is fun when Babs mops.

Mom wants Babs to mop.

Dad's Hot Rod

Dad likes Babs to go with him. They go in the hot rod. Dad sits in the hot rod. Babs sits on top. Dad likes his pals to see her.

When they pass his pals Babs yells, "Bip, bop, dop." Dad's pals like that.

Then Babs and Dad go to the hot rod shop. Dad gets pins and nuts for his hot rod.

Dad sits in the hot rod. Babs sits on top.

Sis

Sis likes Babs. I get mad when Babs has a hat on. "'Bots should not have hats. What if she has to set a cup on her top?" I say.

Sis says, "I will get the hat off Babs." And she does.

Then I am not mad.

Sis likes Babs.

Pals

I like when Babs hops. She can hop on top of the dog. The dog is Tam.

Tam does not like when Babs hops on him. Tam gets up when Babs is on him. Then Babs falls on the rug.

I have to pick up Babs when she falls.

The cat is Jen. Jen likes Babs. When Babs hops, Jen goes with her. Babs hops, Jen runs. They have fun.

My pal is Sam. He likes Babs. He likes to have Babs get us pop and chips.

Babs sets the chips on her top. Then she hops to us.

When we have the chips, Babs goes back. She puts pop in a cup. She puts the cup on her top. Then she hops to us.

Mom does not like Babs to do that. If Babs falls then pop gets on the rug. It is a mess. Mom gets mad.

She puts the cup on her top.

Babs does not get mad. Babs gets the mop. Babs mops the mess. She mops up pop. She picks up chips. Then Mom is not mad.

Pals in the Bed

I like when Babs hops. And I like when she naps. She hops on the bed and sits with the cat. The cat and Babs nap in the sun.

Then I get on the bed. I nap with them. Then the dog hops on the bed. He sets his chin on my back.

The cat and Babs nap in the sun.

The cat sits on my legs. Babs goes to my neck. She sits and rubs my neck. Then I nap.

Then Mom and Dad are with us. The dog gets a kiss from mom. The cat gets a kiss from mom. Babs the 'bot gets a kiss.

Mom pats me. "Your pals are in bed with you. That is fun," she says. Then I get a kiss from Mom and a kiss from Dad. I nap with my pals. My cat, my dog, and my 'bot.

Sight Words used in "Babs the 'Bot"

a, and, are, does, for, from, go, goes, have, he, her, his, I, like, likes, my, of, puts, say, says, see, she, the, they, to, wants, we, you, your

Approximately 550 total words

THE CUB

The Cub

The tan cub sits on a log. He can see thick fog. Lots and lots of thick fog. He does not see his mom. She should be here. But she is not.

The cub is sad. What does he want? His mom. He can not see her in the fog.

The Dog

The cub can see a dog in the fog. The dog is at a rock. It is a big tan dog. The dog picks up a log. It is a big, thick log. The dog sets the log on a rock and runs. Then the cub does not see the dog.

The cub sits and sits. He is sad. His mom is not here. He is sad.

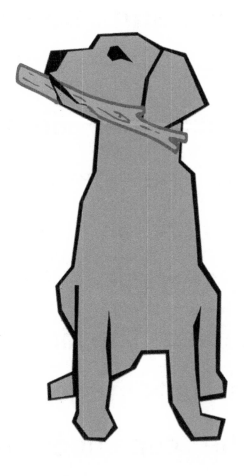

The dog picks up a log.

The Kid and The Man

A kid runs up the path. The path has mud. Lots and lots of mud. The kid has mud on her leg. The kid falls. A man falls in the mud.

The cub does not like the kid. The cub does not like the man.

They could be bad. The cub wants to run from them. The cub wants his mom.

In the Fog

In the fog the cub can see a tan dog. It is big. It is big, big, big.

Then the cub sees what it is. It is not a dog. It is his mom.

His mom does kiss him. He is not sad.

His mom can see the kid and the man. They could be bad. His mom runs up the path. The cub runs with Mom.

It is not a dog. It is his mom.

The cub and his mom run and run. The cub wants a nap. He wants to nap with his mom.

Mom sits on a rock. She can not see the man. She can not see the kid. They do not run to get the cub and mom.

It is OK. The man is not bad. The kid is not bad. The mom does kiss her cub with a lick.

Yum Bugs

Mom picks up a rock. The cub can see bugs. Lots and lots of bugs. Yum! The cub has a lick of bugs. He likes them. Yum, yum, yum.

Then he can not see bugs. He is sad. He would like to have lots and lots of bugs. Mom does lick his chin. He does like his mom.

Mom picks up a rock.

The Van

Mom runs on the path. The cub runs with her. He does wish for bugs.

Mom does not run. She sits on the path. A van is up the path. The cub does not like the van. It could be bad.

A man is in the van. This man has a cap. It is not the man with the kid. This could be a bad man.

The cub sees a box. It is at the back of the van. What is in the box? The cub can tell it is yum. The cub wants to go to the box. The cub wants what is in the box.

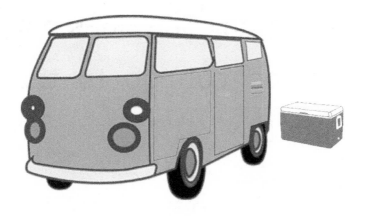

The cub does see a box. It is at the back of the van.

Mom does not like the man. He could be a bad man. She does not let the cub go to the yum box.

The Box

Then the man is not in the van. He is at the box. The man picks up the box lid. He gets a yum from the box.

The man sets the lid on the yum box. He sits on the yum box.

He gets a yum from the box.

The man has a red yum. The cub wants that yum.

The man gets up. He jogs on the path. The man is not at the box. The cub can not see the man.

Mom goes to the yum box. The cub goes with her.

Mom nips the yum box lid. She sets the lid on a big rock.

Mom lets the cub get a yum. The cub gets a yum from the box. Yum, yum.

The cub wants lots of yums. Mom wants lots of yums. They have all the yums.

Yums in the Van

Mom can tell the van has yums.

The cub wants a yum from the van.

Mom hits the van. Mom nips the van. The cub wants a yum. Mom can not get the yums.

Mom hits the van. Mom nips the van.

"Do not hit the van," the man yells.

The cub can see the man. He is mad. He is mad, mad, mad. He runs at mom and the cub. He has a log. The man wants to hit Mom.

Mom runs on the path. The cub runs on the path. The man runs on the path.

The man is mad, mad, mad. Is he a bad man? Or is he a mad man? He is mad.

Mom runs to the top of the hill. The cub runs with her.

The man yells, "Do not hit the van. Do not nip the box. I want what is in the box."

Mom runs and runs.

The cub runs and runs.

The man does not run.

He is on top of the hill.

The man goes back to
the van.

At the Log

Mom sits. The cub sits. Mom does kiss the cub. The cub does kiss mom.

Mom gets up. She goes to a log. She picks up the log. The cub can see bugs. Yum bugs.

The cub licks the bugs. The bugs are yum. The cub has all the bugs. The cub likes the bugs. The cub likes his mom.

Mom does kiss the cub.

Sight Words used in "The Cub"

a, and, are, be, could, do, does, for, from, go, goes, has, have, he, her, here, his, I, like, likes, of, OK, or, see, sees, she, should, the, they, to, want, wants, what, would

Approximately 880 total words

Excerpt from Step 3:

THE SUB IN THE FISH TANK

Step 3
Letter Buddies: ang, ing, ong, ung, ank, ink, onk, unk

Step 3 New Sight Words
as, Mr., Mrs., no, put, their, there, where

Suck the Gunk

Jan likes the fish tank. The fish sink and dunk then go to the top. The big red fish has a gal pal. His pal is not red. She is tan. The pink fish likes to hang at the rocks and logs.

The fish sink and dunk then go to the top.

"We should suck the gunk from the tank. The fish do not want yuck and gunk in their tank. Would you do it with me?" Mom says.

"Yes," Jan says. "Let me get the big can. We can fill it with the gunk."

Mom sucks the yuck from the tank. Jan has the can for the gunk.

Mom gets all the gunk from the tank. Then she fills the tank from the tap.

In the tank is a chunk of log. It sits with the rocks.

Mom got it at the fish shop. It is for the fish. It is where the fish go when Mom sucks the tank. The fish think Mom can not see them there.

Step 3 Books
- Mr. Bing has Hen Dots
- The Junk Lot Cat
- Bonk Punk Hot Rod
- The Ship with Wings
- The Sub in the Fish Tank

KEYWORD
-all

all

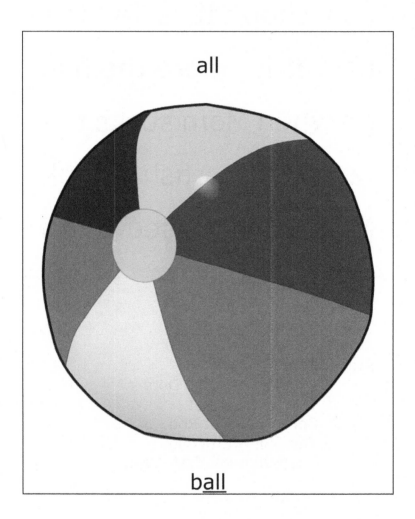

ba<u>ll</u>

DOG ON A LOG Books

Phonics Progression

DOG ON A LOG Pup Books
Book 1
Phonological/Phonemic Awareness:
- Words
- Rhyming
- Syllables, identification, blending, segmenting
- Identifying individual letter sounds

Books 2-3
Phonemic Awareness/Phonics
- Consonants, primary sounds
- Short vowels
- Blending
- Introduction to sight words

DOG ON A LOG Let's GO! and Chapter Books

Step 1
- Consonants, primary sounds
- Short vowels
- Digraphs: ch, sh, th, wh, ck
- 2 and 3 sound words
- Possessive 's

Step 2
- Bonus letters (f, l, s, z after short vowel)
- "all"
- –s suffix

Step 3
- Letter Buddies: ang, ing, ong, ung, ank, ink, onk, unk

Step 4
- Consonant blends to make 4 sound words
- 3 and 4 sound words ending in –lk, -sk

Step 5
- Digraph blend –nch to make 3 and 4 sound words
- Silent e, including "-ke"

Step 6
- Exception words containing: ild, old, olt, ind, ost

Step 7
- 5 sounds in a closed syllable word plus suffix -s (crunch, slumps)
- 3 letter blends and up to 6 sounds in a closed syllable word (script, spring)

Step 8

- Two-syllable words with 2 closed syllables, not blends (sunset, chicken, unlock)

Step 9

- Two-syllable words with all previously introduced sounds including blends, exception words, and silent "e" (blacksmith, kindness, inside)
- Vowel digraphs: ai, ay, ea, ee, ie, oa, oe (rain, play, beach, tree, pie, boat, toe)

WATCH FOR MORE STEPS COMING SOON

Let's GO! Books have less text

Chapter Books are longer

DOG ON A LOG Books
Sight Word Progression

DOG ON A LOG Pup Books
a, does, go, has, her is, of, says, the, to

DOG ON A LOG Let's GO! and Chapter Books

Step 1
a, and, are, be, does, go, goes, has, he, her, his, into, is, like, my, of, OK, says, see, she, the, they, to, want, you

Step 2
could, do, eggs, for, from, have, here, I, likes, me, nest, onto, or, puts, said, say, sees, should, wants, was, we, what, would, your

Step 3
as, Mr., Mrs., no, put, their, there, where

Step 4
push, saw

Step 5
come, comes, egg, pull, pulls, talk, walk, walks

Step 6
Ms., so, some, talks

Step 7
Hmmm, our, out, Pop E., TV

Step 8
Dr., friend, full, hi, island, people, please

More DOG ON A LOG Books

Most books available in Paperback, Hardback, and e-book formats

DOG ON A LOG Parent and Teacher Guides

Book 1 (Also in FREE e-book and PDF Bookfold)
- Teaching a Struggling Reader: One Mom's Experience with Dyslexia

Book 2 (FREE e-book and PDF Bookfold only)
- How to Use Decodable Books to Teach Reading

DOG ON A LOG Pup Books
Book 1
- Before the Squiggle Code (A Roadmap to Reading)

Books 2-3
- The Squiggle Code (Letters Make Words)
- Kids' Squiggles (Letters Make Words)

DOG ON A LOG Let's GO! and Chapter Books

Step 1
- The Dog on the Log
- The Pig Hat
- Chad the Cat
- Zip the Bug
- The Fish and the Pig

Step 2
- Mud on the Path
- The Red Hen
- The Hat and Bug Shop
- Babs the 'Bot
- The Cub

Step 3
- Mr. Bing has Hen Dots
- The Junk Lot Cat
- Bonk Punk Hot Rod
- The Ship with Wings
- The Sub in the Fish Tank

Step 4
- The Push Truck
- The Sand Hill
- Lil Tilt and Mr. Ling
- Musk Ox in the Tub
- The Trip to the Pond

Step 5
- Bake a Cake
- The Crane at the Cave
- Ride a Bike
- Crane or Crane?
- The Swing Gate

Step 6
- The Colt
- The Gold Bolt
- Hide in the Blinds
- The Stone Child
- Tolt the Kind Cat

Step 7
- Quest for A Grump Grunt
- The Blimp
- The Spring in the Lane
- Stamp for a Note
- Stripes and Splats

Step 8
- Anvil and Magnet
- The Mascot
- Kevin's Rabbit Hole
- The Humbug Vet and Medic Shop
- Chickens in the Attic

Step 9
- Trip to Cactus Gulch 1: The Step-Up Team
- Trip to Cactus Gulch 2: Into the Mineshaft
- Play the Bagpipes
- The Hidden Tale 1: The Lost Snapshot

All chapter books can be purchased individually or with all the same-step books in one volume.

Steps 1-5 can be bought as Let's GO! Books which are less text companions to the chapter books.

All titles can be bought as chapter books.

WATCH FOR MORE BOOKS COMING SOON

How You Can Help

Parents often worry that their child (or even adult learner) is not going to learn to read. Hearing other people's successes (especially when they struggled) can give worried parents or teachers hope. I would encourage others to share their experiences with products you've used by posting reviews at your favorite bookseller(s) stating how your child benefitted from those books or materials (whether it was DOG ON A LOG Books or another book or product.) This will help other parents and teachers know which products they should consider using. More than that, hearing your successes could truly help another family feel hopeful. It's amazing that something as seemingly small as a review can ease someone's concerns.

DOG ON A LOG Quick Assessment

Have your child read the following words. If they can't read every word in a Step, that is probably where in the series they should start. Get a printable assessment sheet at: www.dogonalogbooks.com/how-to-use/assessment-tool/

Step 1
fin, mash, sock, sub, cat, that, Dan's

Step 2
less, bats, tell, mall, chips, whiff, falls

Step 3
bangs, dank, honk, pings, chunk, sink, gong, rungs

Step 4
silk, fluff, smash, krill, drop, slim, whisk

Step 5
hunch, crate, rake, tote, inch, mote, lime

Step 6
child, molts, fold, hind, jolt, post, colds

Step 7
strive, scrape, splint, twists, crunch, prints, blend

Step 8
finish, denim, within, bathtub, sunset, medic, habit

Step 9
hundred, goldfinch, free, wheat, inhale, play, Joe

Made in the USA
Las Vegas, NV
17 February 2022